Janae Visits the Art Gallery

By Jennifer Kemarre Martiniello

Library For All Ltd.

DIGITAL EDUCATION
LIBRARY
FOR ALL
FOR THE WORLD

Library For All is an Australian not for profit organisation with a mission to make knowledge accessible to all via an innovative digital library solution. Visit us at libraryforall.org

Janae Visits the Art Gallery

First published 2023

Published by Library For All Ltd
Email: info@libraryforall.org
URL: libraryforall.org

Our Yarning logo design by Jason Lee, Bidjipidji Art

Original illustrations by keishart

Janae Visits the Art Gallery
Kemarre Martiniello, Jennifer
ISBN: 978-1-922991-03-4
SKU01395

Janae Visits the Art Gallery

We respect and honour Aboriginal and Torres Strait Islander Elders past, present and future. We acknowledge the stories, traditions and living cultures of Aboriginal and Torres Strait Islander peoples on this land and commit to building a brighter future together.

Today my class is going
to visit the art gallery.

I am so excited, I can
hardly eat any breakfast.

Dad usually takes me to school, but today he is late.

I get worried that I'll miss the bus taking my class to the art gallery.

Next thing I hear is Grandma say, "Don't worry, Janae, I'll take you to school."

I was so glad. Grandma helps me make my lunch and pack my bag.

I'm four and can dress myself, so I put on my sparkly shoes that Grandma bought me.

Then we get in the car.

I love it when Grandma takes me to school.

She plays nice music that I can jiggle my feet to.

We make it just in time for the bus and the teacher makes sure we are all sitting safely.

I wave goodbye to Grandma.

When we get to the gallery, we see many different and beautiful things that people have made to display.

We all loved the visit.

Dad picks me up and I tell him about the many things we saw.

He is pleased Grandma drove me to school and I got to go to the art gallery.

When we got home,
I told Grandma the best
thing was seeing *her*
artwork in the gallery
and telling all my friends
that my grandma
made that!

You can use these questions to talk about this book with your family, friends and teachers.

What did you learn from this book?

Describe this book in one word. Funny? Scary? Colourful? Interesting?

How did this book make you feel when you finished reading it?

What was your favourite part of this book?

download our reader app
getlibraryforall.org

About the author

Jennifer was born in Adelaide and is from the Arrernte Nation. She lives in Canberra with her family and loves taking them to the art gallery. She loves telling stories and spending time with family.

Our Yarning

Want to discover more books from this collection? Our Yarning is a collection of books written by Aboriginal and Torres Strait Islander peoples across Australia.

We know that children learn better, and enjoy reading more, when they see themselves in the stories, characters and illustrations of the books they read.

To download the app, visit the Google Play Store on any Android device and search 'Our Yarning'.

libraryforall.org

www.ingramcontent.com/pod-product-compliance
Lightning Source LLC
Chambersburg PA
CBHW042350040426
42448CB00031B/3439